FRANCIS FRITH'S

MATLOCK

PHOTOGRAPHIC MEMORIES

ROLY SMITH, president of the Outdoor Writers' Guild and member of the British Guild of Travel Writers, is a freelance writer and editor, and the author of 40 books on walking and the countryside. Based in Bakewell in the Peak District, Roly took voluntary early retirement from his position as Head of Information Services with the Peak District National Park - the busiest in Britain - in May 1997, to concentrate on his freelance career. Previously he enjoyed a 20-year, award-winning career in daily paper journalism, latterly on the *Birmingham Post* and *Evening Mail*. He is vice-president of the South Yorkshire and North East Derbyshire area of the Ramblers' Association.

FRANCIS FRITH'S
PHOTOGRAPHIC MEMORIES

MATLOCK

PHOTOGRAPHIC MEMORIES

ROLY SMITH

First published in the United Kingdom in 2004 by
Frith Book Company Ltd

Limited Hardback Subscribers Edition Published in 2004
ISBN 1-85937-825-0

Paperback Edition 2004
ISBN 1-85937-676-2

British Library Cataloguing in Publication Data

Francis Frith's Matlock - Photographic Memories
Roly Smith

Frith Book Company Ltd
Frith's Barn, Teffont,
Salisbury, Wiltshire SP3 5QP
Tel: +44 (0) 1722 716 376
Email: info@francisfrith.co.uk
www.francisfrith.co.uk

Printed and bound in Great Britain

Front Cover: **MATLOCK BATH**, *Heights of Abraham c1955* M47025
Frontispiece: **MATLOCK**, *Darley Dale, the Pool C1955* D143049

*The colour-tinting is for illustrative purposes only, and is not intended to be his-
torically accurate*

AS WITH ANY HISTORICAL DATABASE THE FRITH ARCHIVE IS CONSTANTLY
BEING CORRECTED AND IMPROVED AND THE PUBLISHERS WOULD WELCOME
INFORMATION ON OMISSIONS OR INACCURACIES

CONTENTS

FRANCIS FRITH: VICTORIAN PIONEER   7

MATLOCK - AN INTRODUCTION   10

CROMFORD   14

MATLOCK BATH   20

HIGH TOR   46

MATLOCK   52

DARLEY DALE   60

THE SURROUNDING VILLAGES   68

INDEX   87

NAMES OF SUBSCRIBERS   88

Free Mounted Print Voucher   91

FRANCIS FRITH
VICTORIAN PIONEER

FRANCIS FRITH, founder of the world-famous photographic archive, was a complex and multi-talented man. A devout Quaker and a highly successful Victorian businessman, he was philosophical by nature and pioneering in outlook.

By 1855 he had already established a wholesale grocery business in Liverpool, and sold it for the astonishing sum of £200,000, which is the equivalent today of over £15,000,000. Now a very rich man, he was able to indulge his passion for travel. As a child he had pored over travel books written by early explorers, and his fancy and imagination had been stirred by family holidays to the sublime mountain regions of Wales and Scotland. 'What lands of spirit-stirring and enriching scenes and places!' he had written. He was to return to these scenes of grandeur in later years to 'recapture the thousands of vivid and tender memories', but with a different purpose. Now in his thirties, and captivated by the new science of photography, Frith set out on a series of pioneering journeys up the Nile and to the Near East that occupied him from 1856 until 1860.

INTRIGUE AND EXPLORATION

These far-flung journeys were packed with intrigue and adventure. In his life story, written when he was sixty-three, Frith tells of being held captive by bandits, and of fighting 'an awful midnight battle to the very point of surrender with a deadly pack of hungry, wild dogs'. Wearing flowing Arab costume, Frith arrived at Akaba by camel sixty years before Lawrence of Arabia, where he encountered 'desert princes and rival sheikhs, blazing with jewel-hilted swords'.

He was the first photographer to venture beyond the sixth cataract of the Nile. Africa was still the mysterious 'Dark Continent', and Stanley and Livingstone's historic meeting was a decade into the future. The conditions for picture taking confound belief. He laboured for hours in his wicker dark-room in the sweltering heat of the desert, while the volatile chemicals fizzed dangerously in their trays. Back in London he exhibited his photographs and was 'rapturously cheered' by members of the Royal Society. His reputation as a photographer was made overnight.

VENTURE OF A LIFE-TIME

Characteristically, Frith quickly spotted the opportunity to create a new business as a specialist publisher of photographs. He lived in an era of immense and sometimes violent change. For the poor in the early part of Victoria's reign work was exhausting and the hours long, and

people had precious little free time to enjoy themselves. Most had no transport other than a cart or gig at their disposal, and rarely travelled far beyond the boundaries of their own town or village. However, by the 1870s the railways had threaded their way across the country, and Bank Holidays and half-day Saturdays had been made obligatory by Act of Parliament. All of a sudden the working man and his family were able to enjoy days out and see a little more of the world.

With typical business acumen, Francis Frith foresaw that these new tourists would enjoy having souvenirs to commemorate their days out. In 1860 he married Mary Ann Rosling and set out on a new career: his aim was to photograph every city, town and village in Britain. For the next thirty years he travelled the country by train and by pony and trap, producing fine photographs of seaside resorts and beauty spots that were keenly bought by millions of Victorians. These prints were painstakingly pasted into family albums and pored over during the dark nights of winter, rekindling precious memories of summer excursions.

THE RISE OF FRITH & CO

Frith's studio was soon supplying retail shops all over the country. To meet the demand he gathered about him a small team of photographers, and published the work of independent artist-photographers of the calibre of Roger Fenton and Francis Bedford. In order to gain some understanding of the scale of Frith's business one only has to look at the catalogue issued by Frith & Co in 1886: it runs to some 670 pages, listing not only many thousands of views of the British Isles but also many photographs of most European countries, and China, Japan, the USA and Canada - note the sample page shown on page 9 from the hand-written Frith & Co ledgers recording the pictures. By 1890 Frith had created the greatest specialist photographic publishing company in the world, with over 2,000 sales outlets - more than the combined number that Boots and WH Smith have today! The picture on the next page shows the Frith & Co display board at Ingleton in the Yorkshire Dales (left of window). Beautifully constructed with a mahogany frame and gilt inserts, it could display up to a dozen local scenes.

POSTCARD BONANZA

The ever-popular holiday postcard we know today took many years to develop. In 1870 the Post Office issued the first plain cards, with a pre-printed stamp on one face. In 1894 they allowed other publishers' cards to be sent through the mail with an attached adhesive halfpenny stamp. Demand grew rapidly, and in 1895 a new size of postcard was permitted called the court card, but there was little room for illustration. In 1899, a year after Frith's death, a new card measuring 5.5 x 3.5 inches became the standard format, but it was not until 1902 that the divided back came into being, so that the address and message could be on one face and a full-size illustration on the other. Frith & Co were in the vanguard of postcard development: Frith's sons Eustace and Cyril continued their father's monumental task, expanding the number of views offered to the public and recording more and more places in Britain, as the coasts and countryside were opened up to mass travel.

Francis Frith had died in 1898 at his villa in Cannes, his great project still growing. The archive he created continued in business for another seventy years. By 1970 it contained over a third of a million pictures showing 7,000 British towns and villages.

FRANCIS FRITH'S LEGACY

Frith's legacy to us today is of immense significance and value, for the magnificent archive of evocative photographs he created provides a unique record of change in the cities, towns and villages throughout Britain over a century and more. Frith and his fellow studio photographers revisited locations many times down the years to update their views, compiling for us an enthralling and colourful pageant of British life and character.

We are fortunate that Frith was dedicated to recording the minutiae of everyday life. For it is this sheer wealth of visual data, the painstaking chronicle of changes in dress, transport, street layouts, buildings, housing, engineering and landscape that captivates us so much today. His remarkable images offer us a powerful link with the past and with the lives of our ancestors.

THE VALUE OF THE ARCHIVE TODAY

Computers have now made it possible for Frith's many thousands of images to be accessed almost instantly. Frith's images are increasingly used as visual resources, by social historians, by researchers into genealogy and ancestry, by architects and town planners, and by teachers involved in local history projects.

In addition, the archive offers every one of us an opportunity to examine the places where we and our families have lived and worked down the years. Highly successful in Frith's own era, the archive is now, a century and more on, entering a new phase of popularity. Historians consider the Francis Frith Collection to be of prime national importance. It is the only archive of its kind remaining in private ownership. Francis Frith's archive is now housed in an historic timber barn in the beautiful village of Teffont in Wiltshire. Its founder would not recognize the archive office as it is today. In place of the many thousands of dusty boxes containing glass plate negatives and an all-pervading odour of photographic chemicals, there are now ranks of computer screens. He would be amazed to watch his images travelling round the world at unimaginable speeds through internet lines.

The archive's future is both bright and exciting. Francis Frith, with his unshakeable belief in making photographs available to the greatest number of people, would undoubtedly approve of what is being done today with his lifetime's work. His photographs depicting our shared past are now bringing pleasure and enlightenment to millions around the world a century and more after his death.

MATLOCK
AN INTRODUCTION

FOR MOST VISITORS travelling up the A6 from the south, Matlock, and in particular the impressive limestone gorge of the Derwent at Matlock Bath, marks their point of entry into the Peak District.

As they pass through the narrow limestone cleft of Scarthin Nick at Cromford and then go past the Georgian red-brick pile of Richard Arkwright's Masson Mill – now the centrepiece of the newly-designated Derwent Mills World Heritage Site – they travel underneath the cable cars and the wooded Heights of Abraham to enter the former spa town of Matlock Bath.

The beetling limestone crags of Wild Cat and High Tor now frown down on road and river, forcing both into a narrow channel; the houses of the town have to cling to the precipitous hillsides up steep and winding lanes. No one can be left in any doubt that they have now left the low-lying Midland shires and entered hill country.

Although most people today would only

DARLEY DALE, *General View c1955* D143055

recognise the two main settlements of Matlock and Matlock Bath, there were once six Matlocks in all, or at least six hamlets which shared the name. They were Old Matlock, Matlock Bridge, Matlock Bank, Matlock Green, Matlock Moor and Matlock Bath. To the modern visitor, however, the two Matlocks are usually the town centred on Matlock Bridge and Matlock Bank, which now includes the headquarters of Derbyshire County Council, and the former spa and inland resort of Matlock Bath.

The name Matlock is significant and entirely appropriate: it comes from the Old English 'meslach', probably meaning 'the oak where the moot was held.' A thousand years later, the county 'moot' in the form of the County Council is still being held there, in John Smedley's palatial former Hydro on Matlock Bank high on the hillside above the modern town of Matlock.

That imposing gorge cut by the River Derwent as it approaches Matlock has been described as 'one of the most spectacular natural features in the Peak District', and in many ways it is more impressive than the much-lauded Dovedale over to the west. The difference is that the Derwent gorge has been more affected by man's influence, threaded as it is by a busy road (the modern A6) and heavily developed.

How the gorge occurred at all is something of a mystery, for the River Derwent could have taken a far easier course by running through the gritstone and shales to the south-east instead of directly into the outcrop of hard Carboniferous limestone at Cromford. Geologists believe that the answer lies in ancient drainage patterns which have been superimposed on the modern landscape. The covering millstone grit and shale

rocks were probably thinner here, because the limestone was folded into an east-west line running from Bonsall to Matlock Bath. Once the river had cut down into the limestone, it was sufficiently set in its course to continue on this old alignment and to cut out the impressive gorge so admired by tourists today.

The massive excavation of the gorge by Nature was followed by excavation by man, as the mineral resources of the Matlock Gorge have been exploited by generations of miners and quarrymen at least since Roman times. There are many reminders hereabouts of 't'owd man', as the old lead miners were known. When the Romans came to this area in the first century AD, they were able to extract the precious, though poisonous, lead ore (or galena) directly from surface workings; their centre for lead production in the Peak District, Lutudarum, still awaits conclusive identification by archaeologists, although it is thought to have been in the Matlock-Wirksworth area.

One of the open-cast lead mines near the summit of High Tor is still known as Roman Cave today – the name perhaps provides an indication of its antiquity. A lead mine at 'Metesforde' (Matlock), thought to be the Nestus Mine, which is now part of the Rutland Cavern show cave on the Heights of Abraham, was mentioned in the *Domesday Book* of 1086. Other show caverns, such as the Masson and Cumberland Cavern (the first to be opened to the public in 1810), also show evidence of the workings of 't'owd man', and the story of lead mining now forms an important part of the public interpretation of the caves.

Limestone quarrying has also been a traditional industry of the Matlock area for many years, alongside lead mining and farming. Most of the large limestone quarries, such as the Cawdor Quarry in Snitterton Road (which is awaiting redevelopment), are now closed; ironically, the waste fluorspar which the limestone and lead industries discarded is now the more valuable substance – it is used as a whitener and as a flux in the steel industry.

Industry came to the Matlock area early: the area around Cromford became one of the cradles of the Industrial Revolution, thanks to a Preston-born barber and wig-maker, Richard Arkwright. This 'bag-cheeked, pot-bellied' inventor came to Cromford in 1771 to build the world's first water-powered cotton mill. It was the power of the River Derwent – which had been described by Daniel Defoe as 'that fury of the river' – and its tributaries, the plentiful supply of cheap labour, and the isolation from the prying eyes of his competitors which had first attracted Arkwright to Cromford.

His first fortress-like mill was set up in Mill Lane, and he later built the red brick Georgian façade of Masson Mill on the A6 Derby Road in 1784. Arkwright was a most enlightened employ-er for his times, and took great pride in the provision of good housing and social facilities for his workers. Cromford became very much a model village for Arkwright's employees, complete with good, purpose-built housing and a grand village square backed by the Greyhound Hotel, which doubled as a village institute.

But eventually it was that isolation from the main arteries of communication, and in particular from the port of Liverpool from whence the raw cotton was imported, which prevented Cromford from becoming a major industrial centre like Manchester and Leeds. Nevertheless, 15 miles of the Derwent valley from Derby to Cromford and Matlock Bath was recently awarded World Heritage Site status by UNESCO, in recognition of its importance as the birthplace of the factory system.

It was the coming of the Manchester, Buxton, Matlock and Midland Junction Railway to Matlock in 1849 which really put Matlock and Matlock Bath on the map as tourist destinations. With connections to the main line at Derby and eventually Manchester, it brought a new wave of

WINSTER, *Main Street c1955* W569003

tourists to the area, among them the Victorian critic and conservationist, John Ruskin. He spent many holidays here as a child with his parents, and described this part of Derbyshire as 'a lovely child's alphabet; an alluring first lesson in all that is admirable'.

Matlock became known in the advertising of the railway companies as 'England's Switzerland' – indeed, some years before, Lord Byron had famously claimed that 'there were things in Derbyshire as noble as in Greece or Switzerland'.

The man who really put Matlock on the map was John Smedley, son of a Wirksworth worsted spinner and hosier, who discovered the benefits of both hydropathic treatment and religion after attending a hydropathic establishment himself at Ben Rhydding, near Keighley in West Yorkshire in 1846. At the time he was suffering from a breakdown after struggling in the textile business following the closure of his father's mill at Lea in 1823, which he had run.

He opened his first hydropathic establishment on what is now known as Smedley Street in Matlock in 1851, and such was the demand that this building soon became inadequate and he pulled it down and built a larger one on the site. By 1867 he was treating over 2,000 patients a year, with the emphasis on the healing qualities of water applied externally through cold showers and mustard baths, and turning as many away. Smedley's was one of several hydropathic establishments which sprung up in Matlock and Matlock Bath at the time, bringing with them increased prosperity and fast-expanding development to the town.

In 1871, Smedley's Hydro was floated as a public limited company, and the buildings were gradually improved and expanded until they became the palatial, mock-Gothic building lit by beautiful stained glass windows which dominates the town today.

Among the great and the good who became Smedley's patients were the musicians Sir Thomas Beecham, Ivor Novello, and Bing Crosby; the comedians Sir Harry Lauder and Sir George Robey; and General William Bramwell Booth, son of the founder of the Salvation Army. Robert Louis Stevenson, the Scottish writer, is supposed to have written his famous novel *Kidnapped* while he was a client at Smedley's Hydro.

Interest in hydropathy declined after the First World War, and the building was requisitioned by the War Department during the Second World War. The introduction of the National Health Service in 1948 was another nail in its coffin, and eventually the Hydro was sold in 1956 to Derbyshire County Council, who made it their headquarters – a role it still performs today.

This collection of photographs from the Francis Frith collection dates mainly from around the turn of the last century, and shows the Matlock area largely as it was before the advent of mass tourism and the coming of the motor car. We take a journey through the area from the south, passing first through Cromford and Matlock Bath, and then under the heights of High Tor into Matlock itself. Then we continue on the Bakewell road through Darley Dale, where Sir Joseph Whitworth, inventor of the screw thread, was to prove as great a benefactor as Arkwright had been, before visiting some of the beautiful surrounding White Peak villages.

CROMFORD

CROMFORD, *The Bridge 1886* 18578

This early photograph of the 15th-century Cromford Bridge shows a shadowy black-coated figure in the foreground fishing in the River Derwent. This view was taken from the downstream side of the bridge where the arches are pointed, whereas on the upstream side, they are rounded.

CROMFORD
Willersley Castle
c1884 16572

The view has the River Derwent in the foreground. It shows the grandiose mock-Gothic Willersley Castle at Cromford, built by the factory pioneer Richard Arkwright between 1782 and 1788 as his mansion and family home. Unfortunately, he never lived there: the castle was burnt down in 1791, and he died before it was rebuilt and finished.

CROMFORD, *Willersley Castle from Cromford Bridge c1884* 16573

Another view from Cromford Bridge of Willersley Castle, this time seen peeping above the trees. A stone on the bridge marks the spot where Benjamin Heywood went straight into the river as he returned home on horseback in 1697, and emerged unscathed.

CROMFORD, *Willersley Castle c1955* C193012

Willersley Castle later became a Methodist guest house, and
some of the guests can be seen on the entrance steps to the left of
this photograph. Today it is still a Methodist conference centre.

▼ **CROMFORD,** *From Harp Edge 1890* 24625

This view from the wooded heights of Harp Edge above Cromford shows Arkwright's Masson Mill in the centre of the picture, with Willersley Rocks above and the River Derwent on the right. The mill was built in 1784; it succeeded Arkwright's first mill in Mill Lane, which was the first water-powered cotton mill in the world.

► **CROMFORD**
General View 1892
31290A

This general view of Cromford was taken from Allen's Hill; it shows the prominent Greyhound Hotel in the centre of the picture, built by Arkwright as part of the model village he planned for his workers at his nearby cotton mill. Beyond Greyhound Square, the centre of the village, is Cromford's millpond, locally known as the Dam.

◀ **CROMFORD**
Mill Weir 1892
31289

This is a river-side view of the huge, crescent-shaped weir constructed above Arkwright's Masson Mill on the River Derwent, with the tree-topped tor of Willersley Rocks filling the background.

▶ **CROMFORD**
The Black Rocks 1892 31294

This view of the overhanging, topmost rocks of the Black Rocks shows some of the many examples of graffiti, some of which is Victorian, which deface the gritstone boulders in the foreground. There are fine views across the Derwent valley from here towards Matlock and Riber Castle.

MATLOCK BATH

MATLOCK BATH, *General View 1886* 18593

This general view of Matlock Bath looks north and shows Smedley's mock-Gothic ruin of Riber Castle on the right horizon, and on the left, the immense limestone crag of High Tor.

▶ **MATLOCK BATH**
General View 1886
18592

In this early view of Matlock Bath, the crocketed spire of the parish church of the Holy Trinity is prominent in the right centre, with the River Derwent on the left. Note the allotments and cultivated terraces spreading up behind the church.

◀ **MATLOCK BATH**
General View 1892
31269a

Another general view of
Matlock Bath, looking up
towards the wooded Heights
of Abraham on the skyline.
The Heights of Abraham were
named by a soldier who
fought with General Wolfe at
his famous victory at Quebec
in 1759.

▶ **CLOSE UP OF 31269A**

MATLOCK BATH
From the Station
1886 18590

From the railway station, we can see how the pretty Derwentside village of Matlock Bath spreads up the wooded hillside. Prominent in the centre of the picture is the spire of the Wesleyan Methodist church, built in 1865.

MATLOCK BATH, *Derwent Terrace c1884* 16545

This view of Derwent Terrace from the south looks towards Riber Castle on the skyline.

MATLOCK BATH
Derwent Terrace
c1864 2094

Another view of Derwent Terrace, this time from the river, with the spire of the Methodist church again prominent in the right centre. The church is now a furniture shop.

MATLOCK BATH, *Derwent Terrace 1892* 31277

This view was taken looking up from the river towards Derwent Terrace. Note the moored boats and boating sheds on the river in the centre, waiting to take tourists for a trip on the Derwent.

MATLOCK BATH, *Derwent Terrace 1892* 31280
Two gaiter-clad gentlemen eye the Frith photographer quizzically
as he sets up for this picture, which was taken on the Promenade.

MATLOCK BATH, *Derwent Terrace 1892* 31276

A deserted Derwent Terrace, with the Jubilee Bridge across the Derwent on the right. This scene would be impossible today, with the busy A6 usually choked with traffic.

MATLOCK BATH
The Promenade 1890
24618

This view of Derwent Terrace again shows the newly-built Jubilee Bridge on the right. It was constructed to celebrate the Golden Jubilee of the reign of Queen Victoria in 1887.

MATLOCK BATH
Jubilee Bridge c1955
M47064

Sixty-five years after No
24618 (page 29) was taken,
the Jubilee Bridge is
decorated with lights for the
annual Matlock Bath
Illuminations, which are
still held every September.
Two lads enjoy a scull down
the Derwent underneath
the bridge.

MATLOCK BATH
The Footbridge 1886
18611

The notice on the cast iron footbridge across the River Derwent was put up by the High Tor Recreation Grounds Company, and advertised the Fern Cave, Lovers' Walks, and the 'Switzerland View'. Matlock and Matlock Bath, by this time a popular tourist destination, was known in the tourist brochures as 'Little Switzerland'. The Midland Railway line runs across the river by the viaduct to the left.

MATLOCK BATH, *The River Derwent Ferry 1892* 31283

Visitors not wishing to use the bridges could enjoy a rowing boat ferry across the river at the time when this photograph was taken. If this photograph is to be believed, there was not much demand for the service!

MATLOCK BATH, *Lovers' Walk 1892* 31284

The tree-lined walks by the side of the River Derwent known as the Lovers' Walks have been popular with visitors since the town became a tourist honeypot in the 19th century. They are still popular today, not least with the groups of leather-suited motorcyclists who have made Matlock Bath their adopted weekend home.

MATLOCK BATH, *Lovers' Walk and the Church 1886* 18607
Another view from the Lovers' Walk, showing the crocketed spire of the parish church of the Holy Trinity across the river.

MATLOCK BATH
The Heights of Abraham c1955
M47007

People gather by the Petrifying Well, outside the Matlock Pavilion. The well and fountain has been used for years to 'petrify' objects placed in it: they eventually become coated with tufa from the lime-rich spring water. In the background, the Prospect Tower at the top of the Heights of Abraham can be seen in the trees – it is now the upper terminus of the famous cable car ride.

MATLOCK BATH, *The Fishpond and the Heights of Abraham c1955* M47052

The Fishpond has been a central feature of Matlock Bath since the village became an important resort and spa in the late 18th and early 19th centuries. The hotel opposite takes its name from the pond.

MATLOCK BATH
South Parade 1892
31274

South Parade was deserted
when the Frith photographer
called. Note the signs on the
right to the Petrifying Wells,
to the boats on the River
Derwent, and to The Royal
Museum, no longer there.

MATLOCK BATH, *South Parade and the Heights of Abraham c1955* M47019

This photograph shows the same scene as No 31274 (pages 36-37) sixty years later, and nothing much has changed apart from tree growth. The trees have been cleared around the Prospect Tower on the Heights of Abraham on the skyline, but the road, now the A6, still seems to be deserted.

MATLOCK BATH
The Heights of Abraham c1955 M47025

This is another view of the main road (the A6) through Matlock Bath.
The wooded Heights of Abraham still form the backdrop. Note
Hodgkinson's Hotel and the Spa Café on the left of the picture, and
the Amusement Arcade, now demolished, on the right.

▶ **MATLOCK BATH**
*The Fishpond
c1955* M47005

Another view of the
Fishpond in the
centre of Matlock
Bath, with visitors
peering in to admire
the exotic goldfish
and carp in the water.

◀ **MATLOCK BATH**
*The Heights of
Abraham from the
Fish Pond c1955*
M47055

This view from the
Fishpond Hotel looks
north towards the
Heights of Abraham.
Note the coach in the
Pavilion car park, and the
increase in the number of
private cars.

▲ **MATLOCK BATH,** *The Grand Pavilion c1955* M47041

The dome-topped Grand Pavilion, originally called the Kursaal, was built on the site of the stables of the Fishpond Hotel by the local council in the 1880s in an attempt to attract the public. Today, it serves as the museum of the Peak District Mines Historical Society and as the Matlock Bath Tourist Information Centre.

◄ **MATLOCK BATH**
The Heights of Abraham c1955
M47037

This view of the Heights of Abraham above Matlock Bath shows the Prospect, or Victoria, Tower. This was erected in 1884 when the heights were opened as pleasure gardens for the public.

▼ **MATLOCK BATH,** *North Parade and the River Derwent c1955* M47038

Looking north across Derwent Terrace and North Parade towards Smedley's Riber Castle on the skyline.

▶ **MATLOCK BATH**
North Parade 1892
31272

A horse and trap (right) wait on North Parade, with the Midland Hotel opposite (left). This photograph was taken from the bridge which goes to the station in the centre of Matlock Bath. The way to the Heights of Abraham and the Prospect Tower runs up Brunswood Road in the centre.

◄ **MATLOCK BATH**
The New Bath Hotel c1955
M47016

This view shows the Georgian façade of the New Bath Hotel, originally known as Mr Tyack's New Bath Hotel. It has served visitors to Matlock Bath for 200 years, and is fed by a warm water spring which supplies a basement plunge pool and an outdoor swimming pool. The original part of the hotel is on the right of the picture, with a later extension to the left.

► **MATLOCK BATH**
The Road to the Temple Hotel c1864
2096

Known as 'Little Switzerland' to generations of tourists, Matlock Bath has long attracted visitors to its craggy limestone gorge cut by the River Derwent. This view looks down on the hillside villas from the road which winds up to the Temple Hotel, which dates from the 1760s.

▲ **MATLOCK BATH,** *From the Pavilion c1900* M47301

Looking towards the distant limestone crag of High Tor and the Derwent gorge from near the Pavilion in the centre of Matlock Bath.

▶ **MATLOCK BATH**
The Heights of Abraham c1955 M47046

This distant view of the Heights of Abraham was taken from the Upperwood area. On the hilltop to the right we can just see the shell of Riber Castle, and in the centre is High Tor.

MATLOCK BATH
The Royal Cumberland Cavern c1955 M47042

The Royal Cumberland Cavern was one of several public show
caves in Matlock Bath during the 1950s, and was well known for
its formations of calcite and traces of the work of former lead
miners. It is no longer open to the public, although visitors can
still go underground at the Great Rutland and Masson Caverns on
the Heights of Abraham.

HIGH TOR

MATLOCK, *The Dale c1955* M273041

This aerial view of the Derwent Gorge, with High Tor on
the left, shows how it was cut through by the river
following the Ice Age. The prominent hill on the skyline
is Crich Stand.

MATLOCK BATH
High Tor c1876 8924

This great, 300-foot vertical wall of limestone formed by the River Derwent as it cut its impressive gorge between Matlock and Matlock Bath is known as High – originally Hey – Tor. This is a very early photograph, taken from the banks of the river.

MATLOCK BATH, *High Tor 1886* 18609

Another view of High Tor taken from an almost identical spot on the Derwent to No 8924 (above) a decade later. Note the weir in the foreground.

▼ **MATLOCK BATH,** *High Tor 1890* 24624

This view is taken from further along the river than No 18609 (page 47). Note the rowing boat moored on the left bank. There have been recreation grounds on the summit of the Tor for many years, and the view from the top is extensive.

► **MATLOCK BATH**
High Tor 1892 31288b

This is a closer view of the beetling limestone crag. Today, the face attracts rock climbers, and contains some of the most severe routes in the Peak District.

◀ **MATLOCK BATH**
High Tor 1892
31286

This more panoramic
view of the tor shows
the winding main
road, now the A6,
which passes beside
the river and beneath
the rocks.

▶ **MATLOCK BATH**
From High Tor
c1955 M47053

This dizzying view from
the summit of High Tor
looks north towards
Matlock. Note how the
road and the river are
sandwiched into the
narrow gorge cut by the
River Derwent
following the Ice Age.
Just beyond the summit
of High Tor are the
open cast lead mines
known as the Fern and
Roman Caves.

▶ **MATLOCK BATH**
High Tor c1955 M47072

This view, taken 60 years after No 31286 (page 49), is almost identical, but it shows the rooftops of the first houses in Matlock in the foreground.

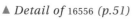

▲ *Detail of* 16556 *(p.51)*

▼ *Detail of* M47072 *(p.50)*

◄ **MATLOCK BATH**
On the Derwent c1884
16556

A series of limestone crags, the highest of which is High Tor, mark the eastern bank of the River Derwent as the traveller progresses towards Matlock. These lower crags include Pic Tor, on which stands the Matlock Bath war memorial, to the left of this photograph.

MATLOCK

MATLOCK
Riber Castle and the River Derwent c1955 M273061

This view from the River Derwent shows John Smedley's folly, Riber Castle, dominating the skyline.

MATLOCK, *Aerial View c1955* M273301

An aerial view of the centre of Matlock, showing in the centre John Smedley's massive Hydropathic Establishment on Smedley Street, which is now the headquarters of Derbyshire County Council.

MATLOCK, *The Winter Gardens, Smedley's Hydro c1955* M273038

Note the potted plants and the wickerwork chairs, with patients enjoying a quiet cup of tea in the sun. The Hydro was sold a year later to the county council.

▼ **MATLOCK,** *Dale Road 1892* 31282

A traffic-free view of Dale Road shows the Victorian Gothic style of the Old English Hotel (right) to good effect. This street scene has changed very little over the last 100 years, and many of the shops in Dale Road are still recognisable.

► **MATLOCK**
The Queen's Head c1870 M273332

This view from the bridge over the River Derwent shows a horse and cart in front of the Queen's Head Hotel (now shops) to the centre left, and the former post office (again now a shop) in the centre.

◄ MATLOCK
The Bridge 1892
31290

Matlock Bridge was originally built in the 16th century, but it was widened in 1903-04 after traffic was found to be queuing up to cross it. This photograph shows the original, older, downstream side.

► MATLOCK
The Square c1870
M273343

Now called Crown Square, this is the modern hub of Matlock, although when this photograph was taken, people could stand with impunity in the centre of the street to have a conversation.

▶ **MATLOCK**
The Town Centre
c1955 M273005

By the mid-Fifties, Crown Square had taken on a much more urban appearance, with black and white kerb markings, a Belisha beacon on the right, and traffic signs in the centre of the roundabout. We are looking up the steep incline of Bank Road, with the fondly-remembered Ormes department store at centre right.

◀ **MATLOCK**
Bank Road c1949
M273004

Another view of Bank Road in the centre of Matlock. Where the man is crossing the road on the left is now a pedestrian-controlled crossing.

▲ **MATLOCK,** *The Park c1955* M273002

Hall Leys Park and Pleasure Gardens were created when the riverside site, formerly water meadows, was purchased by the town council in 1889. It forms an important green space in the centre of the town. Riber Castle stands on the skyline, as it does in so many views of Matlock.

◄**MATLOCK**
Hall Leys Pleasure Gardens c1955 M273025

The ornate bandstand and café in Hall Leys Pleasure Gardens were erected by the town council in 1914.

MATLOCK
Hall Leys Park and Riber Castle c1955
M273060

Another view from the Hall Leys Park, showing the tennis courts in the foreground, the bandstand (right) and Riber Castle on the hillside above.

MATLOCK, *The Boating Lake c1955* M273031

The popular boating lake in Hall Leys Park, seen here being enjoyed by a granddad and his grandchildren, now has ten motor-powered boats.

MATLOCK
Hall Leys Park
c1955 M273062

This view, looking
towards the town centre,
again shows the boating
lake in Hall Leys Park,
this time deserted.

MATLOCK BANK, *General View 1892* 31291

Matlock Bank in the centre spreads up the eastern bank of the Derwent. A mill chimney is prominent to the left, while in
the background is Smedley Hydropathic Establishment, which provided a popular cure for all sort of ills.

DARLEY DALE

DARLEY DALE, *General View c1955* D143053

This distant view was taken from the north of the linear village of Darley Dale, which spreads along the A6 north of Matlock on the road to Bakewell. Riber Castle can be seen on the distant horizon to the left.

DARLEY DALE, *General View c1955* D143055

This is a closer view of Darley Dale, looking towards the solitary
tree-topped Oker Hill, which was the subject of a sonnet by
William Wordsworth published in 1829 about two local lads going
to war, only one of whom returned.

DARLEY DALE
The Church 1892
31305

The mainly Perpendicular parish church of St Helen at Darley Dale is probably best known for its massive 2,000-year-old churchyard yew, seen here on the extreme right.

DARLEY DALE, *The Caravan Park c1955* D143042

As a major southern entrance to the delights of the Peak District, Darley Dale has always catered for visitors. This photograph shows a caravan park in the village, with families enjoying the scenery and fresh air.

DARLEY DALE, *The Pleasure Gardens c1955* D143046

This view of the Pleasure Gardens shows the rustic park furniture
which was fashionable at the time - note the seats, the fencing
and the footbridge.

DARLEY DALE, *The Pool c1955* D143049

Dad's position on his inflatable raft on the pool of the Pleasure
Gardens at Darley Dale looks fairly precarious; the rest of the
family look on and shout instructions.

▶ **TWO DALES**
Chesterfield Road
c1960 T206005

This hamlet on the
Chesterfield Road out of
Darley Dale is known as Two
Dales; the name probably
comes from the twin valleys
of Hall Dale and Sydnope
Dale, which run on either
side of the settlement.

◄ **TWO DALES**
Red House c1955
T206014

The mock timbered gables of Red House at Darley Dale are now home to a horse and coaching museum, which runs coach-and-fours through the grounds of nearby Chatsworth House for visitors during the summer months.

THE SURROUNDING VILLAGES

ALDERWASLEY, *The Church c1955* A323002

The Victorian parish church of St Margaret's, Alderwasley stands in the grounds of Georgian Alderwasley Hall, two miles east of Wirksworth in the Derwent valley.

69

ALPORT, *The Mill Bridge c1960* A333024

The Mill Bridge in the pretty hamlet of Alport crosses the River Bradford near its confluence with the Lathkill, three miles south of Bakewell. Alport is one of many candidates for Derbyshire's prettiest small village.

ASHOVER, *Ogston Reservoir c1965* A325041

There is still a thriving sailing club at Ogston Reservoir, near Ashover, just as there was when this photograph was taken. The reservoir occupies a pleasant, tree-lined site in the valley of the River Amber.

BONSALL
St James' Church c1955 B485004

The battlemented spire of St James' parish church rises above the village centre at Bonsall, and its Perpendicular style dates it mainly from the 13th century. There is a beautiful clerestory above the nave.

BONSALL
The Cross c1955
B485013

The steeply-sloping Market Place in the centre of Bonsall is dominated by its 17th-century Market Cross, encircled by 13 gritstone steps. In the background is the King's Head public house, one of a number which slaked the thirsts of generations of the lead miners who formed the majority of the population of this sleepy little limestone village.

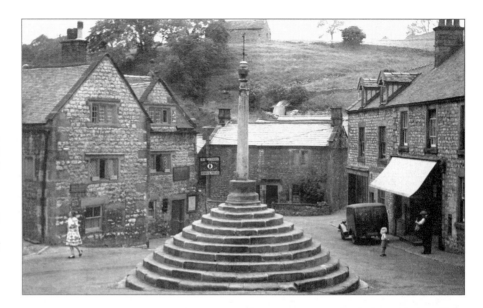

BONSALL, *Via Gellia, the Pig of Lead Inn 1892* 31300

Lead mining was still very much a local industry in Bonsall when this photograph was taken outside the Pig of Lead Inn. The people in the photograph are interesting, from the horse and cart and man carrying a basket and harness on the left, to the two boys, one dressed in a sailor suit, and a man who may be their father in a straw boater in the centre.

BONSALL, *Via Gellia, Tufa Cottage 1886* 18586

Tufa Cottage, on the Via Gellia road from Cromford to Bonsall, was constructed entirely from blocks of tufa, the stone deposited by lime-rich water in this limestone country. A woman poses in her horse-drawn trap (foreground left). The road was named after Phillip Gell of Cromford, who had it built in the late 18th century.

BRASSINGTON
General View c1960
B487016

Brassington lies in the heart of the White Peak lead mining country, and there are many reminders of the work of 't'owd man' – as the lead miners were called – in the surrounding fields. This is a general view showing the limestone cottages of the village.

▼ **CRICH,** *The Stand c1960* C406003

This lighthouse-like monument at Crich was built in 1923 on the 955ft summit of the Stand as a memorial to the men of the Sherwood Foresters who fell in the First World War. The view from the top is outstanding, extending as far as Lincoln Cathedral and the Wrekin in Shropshire.

▶ **ELTON**
The Post Office and the Church c1950
E131013a

Elton is a typical White Peak village, founded on the dual economies of farming and lead mining, and there are many fine 18th-century houses in the village street, some of which we can see here. The pinnacled tower of the parish church of All Saints', reconstructed after the steeple collapsed in 1812, is on the left.

◀ **HOLLOWAY**
Lea Hurst 1892
31296

Ivy-clad Lea Hurst at Holloway, near Matlock, is famous as the home of the Crimean War's 'Lady with the Lamp', Florence Nightingale. This 17th-century gabled house with mullioned windows was greatly enlarged by her father in 1825, and she returned home here after the war in 1856.

▶ **MIDDLETON**
Main Street 1951
M122001

Middleton – its full name is Middleton-by-Wirksworth – was a quarrying and mining village which produced the famous Hopton Wood stone. The narrow and winding Main Street, seen here, is typical of most White Peak villages, and definitely not built for modern traffic.

ROWSLEY
The Peacock Inn
1886 18617

Ponies and traps wait for their passengers outside the 17th-century Peacock Inn at Rowsley, just south of Bakewell on the Matlock road. The Peacock takes its name from the coat of arms of the Manners family from nearby Haddon, and it is a favourite haunt of anglers fishing on the Derwent and Wye, which meet near the village.

ROWSLEY, *The Bridge and the Peacock Inn c1870* 5216

This fine five-arched bridge over the River Derwent at Rowsley has carried traffic for nearly four hundred years. It was built in the early 17th century, and was widened in 1925 from 16 feet to 40 feet to carry the increased traffic on the A6 trunk road between Derby and Manchester. The chimneys of the Peacock Inn can be seen in the background.

SOUTH WINGFIELD
The Church 1892 31304

The 13th-century parish church of All Saints', seen here from the churchyard, lies some way to the east of the village, which is two miles west of Alfreton.

WHATSTANDWELL, *The Valley c1955* W347018

The broad valley of the Derwent near Whatstandwell opens out between well-wooded sides, as we can see in this picture. The valley is shared by the river (on the right), the railway (centre) and the A6 trunk road.

WHATSTANDWELL
The River c1960
W347028

The bridge which carries the A6 over the River Derwent can be seen in the background of this photograph. Whatstandwell gets its strange name from Walter Stonewell, a 14th-century resident whose house was next to the former ford which crossed the river here.

▼ **WINSTER,** *The Old Market House c1955* W569001

The 17th-century Old Market House at Winster was the first property to be acquired by the National Trust in the Peak District, in 1906. The sandstone and brick structure originally had open archways on the ground floor, like the similar building in the centre of Bakewell.

▶ **WINSTER**
Main Street c1955
W569003

Winster is one of the most perfectly-preserved 18th-century villages in the Peak District, as this view shows. Most of the cottages seen here date from that period, when Winster was a prosperous lead mining and farming centre.

◄ **WINSTER**
The View from the Rocks c1960
W569006

Winster Rocks, also known as Wyns Tor, is an outcrop of Dolomitic limestone to the south of the village, on what is now a long distance footpath known as the Limestone Way. The White Peak plateau rolls away in the distance.

► **WINSTER**
West Bank c1955
W569009

West Bank winds up the hill towards the significantly-named Miners' Standard public house on the hill above the village. The 'standard' related to the standard measuring dish for lead, for Winster in its heyday was a lead mining village, and almost every family had someone employed in the industry.

WIRKSWORTH
*Stone Coffins outside
St Mary's Church
c1960* W351003

The 13th-century St Mary's parish church at Wirksworth stands in its own close like a cathedral, and has some of the finest Saxon work of any church in the Peak District. Another feature was the group of stone coffins which stood on the outside wall of one of the nave transepts (centre).

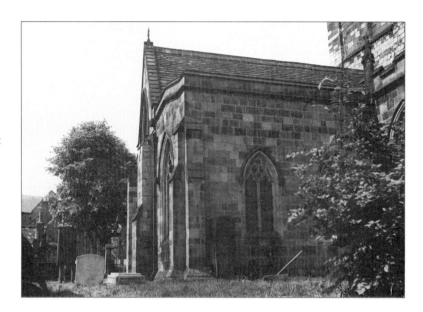

WIRKSWORTH, *Market Place c1965* W351020

The steeply-sloping cobbled Market Place in the centre of Wirksworth was the centrepiece of the restoration of this former lead mining town, which won a Casa Nostra award in the 1980s. Wirksworth was the 'Snowfield' of George Eliot's novel *Adam Bede*.

INDEX

Alderwasley 68-69

Alport 70

Ashover 71

Bonsall 72-73, 74, 75

Brassington 76-77

Crich 78

Cromford 14-15, 16, 17, 18-19

Darley Dale 10, 60-61, 62, 63, 64, 65

Elton 78

Holloway 78-79

Matlock 46, 52, 53, 54-55, 56-57, 58, 59

Matlock Bank 59

Matlock Bath 20-21, 22-23, 24, 25, 26, 27, 28-29, 30-31, 32, 33, 34, 35, 36-37, 38, 39, 40-41, 42-43, 44, 45, 47, 48-49, 50-51

Middleton 79

Rowsley 80

South Wingfield 81

Two Dales 66-67

Whatstandwell 81, 82-83

Winster 12, 84-85

Wirksworth 86

NAMES OF SUBSCRIBERS

The following people have kindly supported this book
by subscribing to copies before publication.

Marlene Ainsworth

Susan Catherine Allen (nee Davis)

E. Bagshaw, Matlock

In celebration of the Baldwin/Elliott Wedding
01/12/03

The Bamford Family, Rotherwood House

Rebecca & Adam Bolton

To a great Grandad, Brian

In Memory of Eileen & Bob Brock

Happy 70th Birthday Paul Brown

Elizabeth & Paul Cutler

Eileen Cutler

David, Sarah, Rhys, Andrew & Jamie

The Davis Family of Rowsley and Matlock

Lewis Lachlan Davis

Gail Gardner, Cromford

Linda Giannas

In Memory of Tom & Dot Gudgeon,
Matlock Bath

Antony J. Handley, Matlock

Mr M. K. Hands

Robert James

Mary Johnson

The Jones Family, Matlock Bath

Amanda, Darren & Libby Lowe

V. McCann, Matlock Bath

C. McCann, Matlock Bath

Christine & Geoff Mockford

Frank Morgan

William Morris, Christmas 2004

Peter J. Naylor, Cromford

Memories of Maurice (Moe) Niven, Matlock

Roger Palin, Matlock

In Memory of G. H. Payne

Simon, Ruth & Amy Rankin

Keith Richards, Matlock Bath

Scott & Phillippa Roe

Andreas & Amilia Santori

Kay Anne Shooter (nee Dinnewell)

In Memory of Mark Skipper (Skip)

The Smith Family, Matlock

Gillian & David Sprakes, Cromford

Joyce & Charles Stennett of Holloway

Claire & Simon Tarrier

The Thompson Family, Matlock

The Thompson Family

Michael & Susan Tomlinson

In Memory of Edna Twort

David & Rita Wellman-Riggs

In Memory of Mavis White, Darley Dale

The Williamson Family, Darley Dale

Mr W. J. Wright, Cromford

FRITH PRODUCTS & SERVICES

Francis Frith would doubtless be pleased to know that the pioneering publishing venture he started in 1860 still continues today. Over a hundred and forty years later, The Francis Frith Collection continues in the same innovative tradition and is now one of the foremost publishers of vintage photographs in the world. Some of the current activities include:

Interior Decoration

Today Frith's photographs can be seen framed and as giant wall murals in thousands of pubs, restaurants, hotels, banks, retail stores and other public buildings throughout the country. In every case they enhance the unique local atmosphere of the places they depict and provide reminders of gentler days in an increasingly busy and frenetic world.

Product Promotions

Frith products are used by many major companies to promote the sales of their own products or to reinforce their own history and heritage. Frith promotions have been used by Hovis bread, Courage beers, Scots Porage Oats, Colman's mustard, Cadbury's foods, Mellow Birds coffee, Dunhill pipe tobacco, Guinness, and Bulmer's Cider.

Genealogy and Family History

As the interest in family history and roots grows world-wide, more and more people are turning to Frith's photographs of Great Britain for images of the towns, villages and streets where their ancestors lived; and, of course, photographs of the churches and chapels where their ancestors were christened, married and buried are an essential part of every genealogy tree and family album.

Frith Products

All Frith photographs are available Framed or just as Mounted Prints and Posters (size 23 x 16 inches). These may be ordered from the address below. From time to time other products - Address Books, Calendars, Table Mats, etc - are available.

The Internet

Already fifty thousand Frith photographs can be viewed and purchased on the internet through the Frith websites and a myriad of partner sites.

For more detailed information on Frith companies and products, look at these sites:

www.francisfrith.co.uk
www.francisfrith.com
(for North American visitors)

See the complete list of Frith Books at:

www.francisfrith.co.uk

This web site is regularly updated with the latest list of publications from the Frith Book Company. If you wish to buy books relating to another part of the country that your local bookshop does not stock, you may purchase on-line.

For further information, trade, or author enquiries please contact us at the address below:
The Francis Frith Collection, Frith's Barn, Teffont, Salisbury, Wiltshire, England SP3 5QP.
Tel: +44 (0)1722 716 376 Fax: +44 (0)1722 716 881   Email: sales@francisfrith.co.uk

See Frith books on the internet at www.francisfrith.co.uk

FREE MOUNTED PRINT

Mounted Print
Overall size 14 x 11 inches

Fill in and cut out this voucher and return
it with your remittance for £2.25 (to cover postage and handling). Offer valid for delivery to UK addresses only.

Choose any photograph included in this book.
Your SEPIA print will be A4 in size. It will be mounted in a cream mount with a burgundy rule line (overall size 14 x 11 inches).

Order additional Mounted Prints at HALF PRICE (only £7.49 each*)
If you would like to order more Frith prints from this book, possibly as gifts for friends and family, you can buy them at half price (with no additional postage and handling costs).

Have your Mounted Prints framed
For an extra £14.95 per print* you can have your mounted print(s) framed in an elegant polished wood and gilt moulding, overall size 16 x 13 inches (no additional postage and handling required).

---

* IMPORTANT!

These special prices are only available if you order at the same time as you order your free mounted print. You must use the ORIGINAL VOUCHER on this page (no copies permitted). We can only despatch to one address.

Send completed Voucher form to:
The Francis Frith Collection, Frith's Barn, Teffont, Salisbury, Wiltshire SP3 5QP

CHOOSE ANY IMAGE FROM THIS BOOK

Voucher for **FREE** and Reduced Price Frith Prints

Please do not photocopy this voucher. Only the original is valid, so please fill it in, cut it out and return it to us with your order.

Picture ref no	Page no	Qty	Mounted @ £7.49	Framed + £14.95	Total Cost
		1	Free of charge*	£	£
			£7.49	£	£
			£7.49	£	£
			£7.49	£	£
			£7.49	£	£
			£7.49	£	£

Please allow 28 days for delivery

* Post & handling (UK)	£2.25
Total Order Cost	£

Title of this book . . . .

I enclose a cheque/postal order for £ . . . .
made payable to 'The Francis Frith Collection'

OR please debit my Mastercard / Visa / Switch / Amex card
(credit cards please on all overseas orders), details below

Card Number

Issue No (Switch only)   Valid from (Amex/Switch)

Expires   Signature

Name Mr/Mrs/Ms . . . .

Address . . . .

. . . .

. . . .

. . . . Postcode . . . .

Daytime Tel No . . . .

Email . . . .

Valid to 31/12/05

Would you like to find out more about Francis Frith?

We have recently recruited some entertaining speakers who are happy to visit local groups, clubs and societies to give an illustrated talk documenting Frith's travels and photographs. If you are a member of such a group and are interested in hosting a presentation, we would love to hear from you.

Our speakers bring with them a small selection of our local town and county books, together with sample prints. They are happy to take orders. A small proportion of the order value is donated to the group who have hosted the presentation. The talks are therefore an excellent way of fundraising for small groups and societies.

Can you help us with information about any of the Frith photographs in this book?

We are gradually compiling an historical record for each of the photographs in the Frith archive. It is always fascinating to find out the names of the people shown in the pictures, as well as insights into the shops, buildings and other features depicted.

If you recognize anyone in the photographs in this book, or if you have information not already included in the author's caption, do let us know. We would love to hear from you, and will try to publish it in future books or articles.

Our production team

Frith books are produced by a small dedicated team at offices in the converted Grade II listed 18th-century barn at Teffont near Salisbury, illustrated above. Most have worked with the Frith Collection for many years. All have in common one quality: they have a passion for the Frith Collection. The team is constantly expanding, but currently includes:

Paul Baron, Jason Buck, John Buck, Ruth Butler, Heather Crisp, David Davies, Isobel Hall, Julian Hight, Peter Horne, James Kinnear, Karen Kinnear, Tina Leary, Stuart Login, David Marsh, Sue Molloy, Glenda Morgan, Wayne Morgan, Kate Rotondetto, Dean Scource, Eliza Sackett, Terence Sackett, Sandra Sampson, Adrian Sanders, Sandra Sanger, Julia Skinner, Claire Tarrier, Lewis Taylor, Shelley Tolcher, Lorraine Tuck and Jeremy Walker.